On Occasion

Selected Poems, 1968-1992

Mary Pryor

A Dacotah Territory Book
Published at Moorhead State University

Distributed by Plains Distribution Service, Inc.
P.O. Box 931
Moorhead, MN 56561

ISBN 0-941127-12-5

ACKNOWLEDGEMENTS

Poems in this collection have been selected by Mark Vinz and Thom Tammaro from Mary Pryor's unpublished manuscripts as well as from her previously published chapbook collections:

Jawboning (1973)
No Metaphysics (1974)
The Bicycle in the Snowbank (1980)
The Song of the Vowels (1985)
My Disrespects (1989)
Face Painter (1989)
Rondeau (1990)

Individual poems in this collection have been published in *AAUP Bulletin, Anachronisms, Bloodroot, Dacotah Territory, The Mainstreeter, Red Weather,* and *The Tenth Muse.*

Poems appear in approximate chronological order, listed years marking beginnings—poems being unfinished until printed, and sometimes later.

Dacotah Territory Press gratefully acknowledges the Moorhead State University Alumni Association for a grant which has made possible the publishing of this book.

CONTENTS

INTRODUCTION

The title Mary Pryor has chosen for this collection puts us on notice that she thinks of herself as an occasional poet, that is, one who announces or celebrates occasions, chiefly public, often events that do not absolutely demand a poetic response. Wearing the poet laureate's mantle, some of the greatest English poets have, occasionally, written occasional poems, as have some of the dreariest English poets, likewise mantled, celebrating the births of princesses or the marriages of princes.

"Poem to Dedicate a Building" is, of course, an occasional poem, but, reading it, we realize that the label isn't, after all, a very useful one. The merely occasional poem is one in which the occasion dominates from the first line to the last, and if we may admire the poet's delicacy or wit or, perhaps temerity, it is, finally, eminently forgettable, for we have read it without that sense of discovery, that brush with truth, that brings us back, over and over again, to poetry.

It is the promise of discovery, a promise she always keeps, that gives so much pleasure to the reading of these poems of Mary Pryor. The special quality of that pleasure comes, I think, from the fact that this journey of discovery leads us through ordinary days, full of ordinary events, occasions, transformed by a far from ordinary imagination.

A good many of these ordinary days were spent on the Moorhead State University campus, and the campus has provided her with many of her subjects in poems treasured by her colleagues, most of such poems escaping inclusion in this collection. She came to Moorhead in 1964, several years before the first poem in this collection, although she had already published a few poems. She had graduated from Grinnell College, where she majored in English and was elected to Phi Beta Kappa. She earned a master's degree at the Yale

School of Nursing, enrolling as well for courses in the Yale School of Drama. After several years as a nurse, she yielded to the call of literature, and took her doctorate at the University of Nebraska, specializing in Renaissance literature. She then came to Moorhead where she remained until her retirement this year, having served, for a time, as chair of the Department of English, and for all her years here, as a wise and supportive member of the university community.

And as someone who noticed things. If she trained her skeptical eye and her mildly, mostly, satiric tongue, on the meretricious fruits of modern life, it was only the dishonesty of political leaders that gave angry passion to her satire. For she is a poet of celebration of the quotidian world that all of us share, giving due attention to absurdity, but proclaiming the loveliness of nature, of gardens, of streets, of prairie, in the lives of the old, in the activities of the young, in customs and memories, of things, all sorts of things; and reminding us of what fills the loveliness of existence with poignancy: grief, disappointment, small threats, large dangers.

She is not afraid of rhymes, not afraid to forego them. She is a poet of the image, exact, resonant, and often unexpected, and of metaphor, and, above all, of wit. There is, since the poems are right here to be read, not much point in quotation, although a hundred lines clamor for attention. I think, for instance, of the growers of sugar beets who "grimly concentrate/the honey of the earth from muddy rind."

Reading these poems, one makes the great discovery that our lives have been richer than we knew, and that, if life deserves our gratitude, so does the celebration of it.

Roland Dille, President
Moorhead State University

On Occasion

RED RIVER PEOPLE

Here on the ridgepole of the continent
where rivers amble north against their kind,
transplanted Scandinavians resent
the glossing tongue, approve the Loki mind.
Shrewd, self-contained, they plow and reap, resigned
to eight-month winter, grimly concentrate
the honey of the earth from muddy rind.
By raising beets they live—to legislate
and make their winter sport political debate.

1968

GARAGE SALE

All summer long in double-stall garages
among the dense-plied lawns and wren-rinsed foliage
the burgers sell to one another rummage:
old wading boots and floor lamp and commode,
electric fry-pan lacking teflon lining,
a high chair, frocks outgrown, the vase bestowed
by Aunt Amanda on the wedding couple,
a jacket (suede, denuded but still supple),
a chiming clock, a grinder, bamboo blinds,
pink china poodle—each to his own taste.

These frugal hedonists have met mankind's
ultimate test—recycling the waste.

1969

RADIO AND ROOT BEER

Our first radio
munched summer
static, listening athletic
leaping-frog from croak to image
homemade root beer bronzing sugar
in the herbal crock's aroma
blending dissonance and drama
mason jars red rubber collared
snapped and sealed inverted on the
iron coal range newsprint layered—
leak? or burst? or quenching thirst?—
and on the air
The Man with the Golden Brain.

A naïve story: man in love
with girl in love with luxury
he buys and buys until beside
a counter, with a satin mule
in hand—"How much?"—he sighs. Among
the matted curls, the fingers grope,
offer—"But sir. What ails the man?"—
serum and golden dregs.
A sound
effect.
A slipper falls and then
a body.

Being maybe five
I merely reasoned that it takes
some brain to stay alive, nor dreamed
that artists were peculiarly imperiled,
nor figured out for adult decades why
root beer brings to mind F. Scott Fitzgerald.

1970

EXORCISM

The dean, the dean,
the brand-new dean,
he taketh the college
for his demesne.
He raiseth Cain
and he sweepeth clean;
he sifteth staff
through a fine-mesh screen.
He instituteth
a new routine.

A martinet
and a crack marine,
wherever he walketh
he spreadeth spleen.
To get attention
he maketh scene:
"There'll be no more travel'n
lecture fee'n,
no more classroom
absentee'n,
no more coffee
and damn little pee'n."

You'll teach all day
and research between.

When address'n the dean,
just keep agree'n
or Ichabod goes
to the guillotine.

The retention committee
will now convene.

Oh, he'll cook your goose
in *haute cuisine*
and set you adrift
in a soup tureen
or begging pennies
with a tambourine.

There are Ph.D.'s
in the bush to glean.
For the staff in hand,
he cares not a bean.

The brand-new dean,
he sweepeth clean.
He sifteth the staff
through a fine-mesh screen:
interchangeable gear
for the teaching machine.

1971

THE DAY THEY TORE DOWN

"Fargo-Moorhead Once Was 'Sin City,'" *Forum*, Centennial Section 6-1, June 15, 1975.

The day they tore down the old whore house
the community flocked to the razing.
The pillars of taste and the straightest of laced
attended the craning and gazing.

Could it be every door was a mirror,
every baluster, satyr or nude,
that the fireplace tile in Florentine style
bore legends entrancingly lewd?

An age since the Madam departed,
her Ladies deceased or redeemed,
respectable folks shared off-color jokes
but confided to none what they dreamed.

Bald merchants with pouches and paunches
ran barefoot through copious curls.
Forgetting hot flashes, double chins, and moustaches,
plump wives became luscious young girls.

The day they tore down the old whore house
we were justly concerned for their fate:
the initial bathtub in a prairie of scrub
and the only bidet in the state.

1971

GEORGIA O'KEEFFE AT EIGHTY-FOUR

With rocks and bones and brushes in the sun,
adobe walls so weathered and refined
the blood and ocher mesas of the mind
go gamboling and ghostly rivers run
broad in their flood-gouged channels, as begun
the work proceeds, the fiery blue outlined
by bony socket, onyx veins entwined
in rock. The colors radiate and stun.
Between the concept and the canvas, gone
all barrier, so sure the hand, unswerving.
Wakes on a roof . . . the chrysolite of dawn . . .
owns dogs and turkeys . . . little use for words . . .
lives painting, planting, pruning and preserving,
and playing Monteverdi to her birds.

1971

GRAIN ELEVATOR

On the Red River Seed Grain Elevator
pigeons alternate
beading the roof rim
(frieze, no, cornice)
kiting off, flying
or waiting, wrying
their necks, sedate

along the eaves
aloft, sunstricken
absorbed into metallic haze
released, shed shadows
on corrugated siding
dark downward gliding

fall
leaves.

1971

KINDERGARTEN

And in the seventh nightmare
you run a kindergarten
single-handed in Siberia,
a hundred four and five-year-olds
to undress and re-dress
morning and evening
and twice a day for recess,
for ten minutes out of doors
in turtleneck and cardigan
and undersocks and leggings
and oversocks and blazer
and underscarf and muffler
and stocking cap and helmet
and buckle-up galoshes
scrambled on the doormat
and undermitts and overmitts
and "stand still" and "stop that"
and lost mitts and lost wits
and wrong coat and wrong hat
and nose blow and "gotta go"
and "couldn't you have SAID so?"
and "please dear" and "oh the brats!"
packed roly-poly spherical
all giggly and hysterical . . .
and in the eighth nightmare . . . .

1972

WEASEL

Born from the ear of his mother,
small as a grasshopper.

We made him a bed of thistledown in a thimble,
fed him on clover nectar and strawberry seed
crushed in a diamond mortar. The size of a mouse,
he liked to doze in pockets and watch from shoulders.

The day we found the spaniel dead on the hearthrug,
a small incision over the jugular,
we held a family council, turned him out.

Missing him rather,
we were noncommittal when neighborhood cats disap-
        peared,
then a Great Dane, then a pony. Rumors fly
of a huge entity raiding peripheral farms
for livestock—and not adverse to man.

1972

DRIVING TO FARGO

Driving to Fargo to donate a pint of blood
windshield veined
wiper blades lazy
Red Owl market sign
oozing anemic neon
tires guzzling
westward over the bridge,

crossing the Red River, a red river
delta myself
raveling westward, seaward,
murmuring sea-words
mirroring shelf and levee
watersheds enmeshed
mutual embankments,

passing the ring-dance willow,
the blond brick luxury barracks,
high-rise thumbing skyward
livid chocolate and salmon,
the Fargo Iron foundry
pipefitters' zoo, the tunnel,
left turn, downtown, through town
arterial pulse of streetlights.

Corpuscles dance
in elastic channels,
wild red bulls
of one's own Pamplona,
till a barricade yields,
till a canula stabs.
"Relax.
Squeeze the bar every five seconds."

Tributary and channel,
rapids and bars and reaches
mirroring shelf and levee
the bole of the ring-dance willow
a carol of naked graces
beetfield, grainland, marshland,
tressel and dock and mill-yard,

nebula rising, downpour,
I join the rain on my windshield
conspiracy of oceans,

caper in veins of strangers
undermining a hostile shore
toward the overthrow of prose.

Now and again someone
befuddled by anaesthetic
awakens alive
and babbles . . . in metaphor.

1973

IF THE NEWS

If the news flashed
that within the next eight hours
the sun would explode
one might
go into hysterics
run for the nearest cathedral
organize an orgy—
but first I should finish the poem.

If the news flashed
that the oil of the Middle East
was all ablaze
the Mediterranean carrying USA's
and USSR's fleets on collision courses
apocalypse galloping in
on all four horses—
first I should finish the poem.

If the news flashed
that a manicured male finger
was depressing the crimson button,
the buried silos sprouting,
nuclear-powered whales
spouting multiple warheads—
first I should finish the poem.

If the news flashed
Chicago reduced to a crater,
the haze on the round horizon radioactive,
underground shelters
gunning down applicants—
first I should finish the poem.

If my bones turned chalk
and my hair were shed like straw,
the flesh of my fingers
rolling off like a glove—
first I would finish the poem.

If I knew that no book, no document,
no film, no tape, no hologram,
no inscription on granite, concrete,
steel, quartz, diamond,
in any human tongue of the past or present
would carry a single phoneme
to eyes or ears or mind
terrestrial or extraterrestrial—

first I would finish the poem.

1973

SAYINGS

Forgiveness is divine

> says the benign old dictator
> watching from under an awning
> while a firing squad
> teaches dissident students
> the vectors of power.

Moderation in all things

> says the humane old industrialist
> rising from a ten-course dinner—
> plate, crystal, flowers, and repartee—
> while around the bonfires strikers
> make broth of old leather.

Beauty is as beauty does

> says the charitable grande dame
> fresh from her fourth face lift
> and a month at the health spa,
> passing an employed mother
> toothless at twenty-five.

"The mills of the gods," say the paving
blocks;

"Grind slowly," remarks the sand;

and the dust, "But exceeding fine."

1973

DESIGNING WOMAN

A woman designed by a man
is a household appliance,
a dishwasher, freezer, wash-drier
with microwave oven,
a recliner with vibrating cushions
and heat in the coils.

A woman designed by a man
is Eve, Mary, Delilah,
Griselda, Leonore-Fidelio,
Beatrice, Gretchen,
Brunhilda, and Helen, and Cleo
with grace in her toils.

Designed by a woman,
a woman is mother superior,
dowager empress,
or prophetess rich in the lore
of her tribe, is a brewer
of potions and broths and intrigues,
and if Eve nibbled apples
her cider recycles the core.

Designed by a woman,
a woman is Eleanor Roosevelt,
aggressively good, a community resource, a blessing,
Florence Nightingale, Golda Meir, and Elizabeth First,
but to any incompetent dreamer
profoundly depressing.

A woman designed by herself,
neither mother nor daughter
nor sister nor wife
nor a dream
to dissolve when the dreamer
undreams her or wakes,

wide awake
dreams herself
and in selfhood
devises an order,
an order, a dream,
and a dancing,
a woman designing—

she dances herself
into being.

1975

URBAN RENEWAL

I mourn for crumbling cornices and curbs,
the ripe autumnal stones of urban blight,
the russets, roses, golds, the sands and bones
razed and replaced—aseptic white-off-white.

Where rectilinear facades prevailed,
new curvilinearities compete.
We bank and shop in spacecraft, winged and tailed,
aesthetic as a plastic potty seat.

Those midnight hours when parking lots are void,
no ghostly townsfolk stroll these glacial flats,
no roisterers or tradesmen, unemployed
ladies who trolled in hansom cabs—all that's
been bulldozed: ghost, tradition, all dispersed,
bare as the sun-bleached geometric fronts
of some Fellini film-set where one hunts
a lost love, photogenic and accursed.

1975

POEM TO DEDICATE A BUILDING

Read at The Center for The Arts,
Moorhead State University, Feb. 20, 1979.

Awake all night . . . easy to think oneself
the only watcher in a sleeping world

easy to think our world the one green eye
observant in a mindless universe,
easy, but self-important . . .
to presume . . . .

"Hello" and "are you there . . . out there . . . out there?"
So far, so good.
Then wait.

Two centuries gone by, comes
"Yes, hello . . . hello yourself . . . yourself . . . yourself . . . ."
Our self?
Two centuries?

Our turn to ask . . . or tell,
mail duplicated letters to the stars?
Old magazines for cosmic waiting rooms?

The topless summit.
How Cambodia fell.
The Shah's vacation. Extra-uterine
conception. What to do with nuclear waste.

History? Science? Great Ideas?

The Death of God.
Trust no one over thirty.
Transactional analysis.
Cost-benefit accounting.
The bottom line.

The Superbowl, two centuries displaced?
Embarrassment to all concerned.

But Lewis Thomas recommends
"Bach, all of Bach"
beamed outward "into space
over and over again . . . .
bragging, of course . . . ."

Technology permitting, then Cezanne,
his "demonstrations that an apple is . . .
part [flesh], part earth."

And then in bronze,
some dark, volcanic birth
sculpture by Baskin
neither paradigm
nor image,
form . . . for what a form is worth.

Then let an actor mime
a clown trapped in the shrinking cage of time . . .
exploding vast of time?

The ebony mask
the elephant in jade
the ikon, gold leaf overlaid,
speak . . . from antiquity.
We . . . understand.

And here within these walls
where tyro actors, artists, and musicians enter,
here watching from our lone galactic beach,
instead of scratching alphabets in sand,
we borrow from our . . . language center

the verbs
of interplanetary . . . speech.

1978

WHOEVER LEFT THE BICYCLE?

Whoever left the bicycle in the snowbank
chained to the pipe-framed bike rack
empty stanchioned
but for this one abandoned and absurd
poor beast?
No playground rattletrap,

a ten-speed racer
handles taped and curled
inward like mountain rams' horns.

Furred with frost
then tire deep
then weedy spokes implanted,
one pedal gone
then axles—
blizzard blended
the fenders join
the oceanic contours
of white.

Saddle and handlebars
alone forge shoreward,
brake cables arching,
defying the undertow.

Vertical sun rays,
drifts involuting:

surfacing
landward
bright fenders porpoise-backed
planing the whitecaps,
radiant spokes
starfish gears,
left pedal, right pedal—

steed,
from what subcontinent
do you return?
Across what glacial
tundras have you wheeled
your serpentining tires?
Dare you come home?

What have you done with your rider?

1979

GRANDMOTHER

The oatmeal bowl,
blue, with the crackly patina,

retrieved from the empty farmhouse
of the grandma I never met,

shelved, forgotten,
later found and used,
never with guests—
for them, the gray Danish—
but solitarily,

lemony sun straining
through the willow's vertical lattice,
a contrail unraveling on blue Formica,
paler than the oatmeal bowl

which I now notice
suffers a hairline fracture,
firm but penetrating.
Revealed as the milk line ebbs,
it jags from base to brim:
chin, lips, nose,
forehead—
a cameo likeness.

1980

BRICKWORK

Behind the old potato warehouse
molting its three-ply masonry
on the gray late January Saturday afternoon
a pair of snow-mobile suits
are harvesting brick

one by one from a heap of frozen rubble
hefting, knocking, scanning
for fissures or blunted corners

clanging a claw hammer
on crusted mud and mortar

hurling the culls on a pile
arraying the chosen
layer by layer, a sort of altar

native clay, of two veins: common
earth-apple fire-stone and antique creamy
mellowed and smoked, for a hearth or a path

in a garden.

Warm brick, chilling work, on the north face
of the old potato warehouse—
"Really lame you tomorrow!"—

but gratifying—
to born collectors
of stones, shells, acorns, pine cones
handsels pleasant to fondle,
anything intricate, shining.

Warped to the worship of obsolescence
keepers of nuclear waste
in the twilight of mutual deterrence

still salvaging brick

invoking our packrat gods?

1984

JAPANESE GARDENS

Photograph by Virginia Barsch

In Japanese gardens
small water
deploys distance.

Space, interrupted,
continues.
Behind bamboo-planted promontory
extends the strait to all ocean.

Nothing is straight,
or random,
or vulgarly blooms:
paint-brush pine,
plumy rushes,
laciniate maple leaves,
the chiseled prow of the roof,
the corners mitered
from reeds of rosy cedar
in the hovering eaves.

White sand raked
by wind, waves,
crows' feet, serpents,
balletic moles
foils a chosen rock.

Reflection doubles the bridge,
a wide oval,
a quiet "Ah."
Shadows of carp fly.

The house floats.

We fold our knees and elbows
between the sky—and sky.

1984

IMMIGRANTS PHOTOGRAPHED

In the apparel of old gentlemen,
Old ladies: hard black serge, dark hats with brims,
and multifolded shawls, shielded with bundles,
buttressed by trunks with camelbacks and hand
carved chests, the destination badly spelled
burnt in the wood, they gaze straight out. They never
smile or meet your eyes but sight along
steel track to where the railroad czars saw fit
to plot a settlement: one guest house, treeless
moorlands—parched, windswept, frozen, burned.
In antique costume, like child dolls with peachskin
faces that peer from under felted rims
and pleated shawls, transported for no fault,
they show no hope, no fear, knowing one backward
glance . . . turns you to salt.

1984

WILLOWWARE

Importunate—a wild word.
Portulaca, portcullis, portmanteau,
"the porches of the ear,"
the ear of the shell,
whorls,
mother-of-pearl—
to which porcelain is piggish.

I own a bit of common willowware
less than a square inch,
parallelogram
with softly rounded corners
buffed and ground
by north Pacific waters
beached
on Orchis Island
off Seattle somewhere.

I'd wear it on a chain
but, rarely wearing
trinkets, I stored it
in a blue glass bowl
of frozen effervescence
lately broken:

the china shard, intaglio, preserved
precious, imponderable.

1984

IN PRAISE OF QUIET

In praise of quiet
all the lovely buttons,
the levers, switches, knobs that quell the yammer
by dimming, tuning down, and turning off—
the chambers of the inner ear reserved,
a charm upon the anvil and the hammer.

In praise of quiet
braided rugs and Persian
carpets, acoustic tile, and weatherstripping,
all damaged doorbells, all uncradled phones.
Praise broken televisions, the reversion
of snowmobile to skis, the eerie pauses
in blizzard—neither wind nor traffic—
churches in silent prayer and football crowds
with total laryngitis, children raiding
cookies, librarians, hospital zones.
Praise trumpet mutes and earmuffs.

Praise to the sound of snow engaging fur,
the sneeze of the amoeba, to the jangle
of bluebells, to the love calls of giraffe,
the murmur of apricots ripening—
the spider on the web my favorite harpist—
the eloquence of holding hands.

Come where, as to our ears a supersonic jet is,
to theirs, a pocket watch.

The denizens of quiet
communicate by eyebrow,
taffeta petticoats all under arrest,
corduroy britches in exile,
bubblegum, popcorn,
and rice crispies outlawed;
police cruiser, fire engine,
and ambulance announced by subtitles.

Once a year in Mardi Gras abandon,
in mutual mad license, all together,
we snap our fingers—
once.

1984

PRAIRIE

Oh . . . here and there a shred,
some lost bandanna
between the soybeans and the golfing greens;
the old north forty and the back nine,
secret, and incognito.
Fossilized? Not so.
Alive, alive, alive, and bona fide.
The rabbits know; and deer, and bobolinks
that orb their domesticity with song,
all bearers of white flags, but no surrender,
canny survivors . . .
prairie too, but more
at risk: no wings, no paws.

Yet, here it is:
true child of fire.
The tame plants cauterized, the phoenix flaunts
great bluestem, goat's beard, meadow rue,
puccoon, and flea bane, paint brush—gold or orange—
and prairie smoke like incense, lavender.

A patch of prairie . . .
is a contradiction.
Prairie means distance.

Does it?
Space derives
from a horizon, what is there or isn't:
sand willow shrubbing west and south, the rest
black willow and burr oak brimming the gullies
notched by the zigzag river.

Standing here
we see a planet
in a ring: scrub willow,
the topknots of the oaks,
the concave ether
and timeless vistas of interior grass.

1984

VENUS IN JANUARY

Working overtime
the air traffic controller
in the glass jar
on the flatlands of Omaha or Fargo
at dusk just going indigo, snow
green gloaming, low
in the south south-west
acknowledges
the oblong laser of Venus
paling all lights to marsh-glow

answers the unintelligible static

and clears her for landing.

1985

REDEEMER

In the eight-storied east tower atrium
of Chicago's Hyatt Regency
where cocktail gardens hang on balconies
float on lilypads in the coin-toss lagoon,
vertically interlaced with reciprocal escalators
and spiral ramps, the air exploding with tinfoil
(a pyramid of multicolored globes
honoring the annual rebirth of Mammon),
the armchaired drinkers embowered in palms,
fig trees, and poinsettias,
and the dapper pianist at the bone-white Yamaha grand
executing classics;
the victims of sensory overload,
self-dramatization, conference depression
disoriented in the east tower
fail to observe
the street-wise sparrow
that flits to the rim of an urn
under tropical foliage,
ruffles its drab feathers,
gleaner of real crumbs,
appreciating
strawberries in December.

1985

THE EMPEROR IS NUDE

The Emperor is nude, but no one knows,
or if we know the Emperor is nude,
reluctant to articulate so rude
a truth, we fear our being misconstrued
as traitors, soft on communistic foes.

I understand the sycophantic brood,
or those who tailored the Supply Side clothes,
or profiteers who merrily collude,
but how does he keep smelling like a rose
to jobless bankrupt people getting screwed?

To hear the cheers, you'd think Old Teflon hewed
rails or cut cherry trees. Could he expose
more than he has already? Unless cued
for every word, his sayings come unglued.
But what's the difference? Atmosphere and mood
are everything. The myth of Star Wars grows.
The Contras kill. Remember Rudolph's nose.
We lemmings follow anything that glows.
The Emperor is bare. Our brains are stewed.
The Emperor is nude, and no one knows.

Triggered by SDI, the stockpile blows.
Nuclear winter ends that pesky food
surplus. We get exactly what we chose.

1986

ICE FISHING

The shanties mushroom
slums on open ice
haphazard, jerry-built
or tight as drums
tarpaper, lumber, plywood
metal siding
stove pipe akimbo
aerial askew
no landscaping
no grid
nor rhyme nor reason
enmeshed in tire tracks.

Later in the season
from time to time
a four-wheeled drive breaks through
submerges.

Come, you anthropologists
to ponder "village culture"
basic urges
the chase, the kill, sweet sloth
oxymoric fusion
drill hole
drop line
uncap another beer.

Drowned in the ball game
who can hear
the wind's wail
coyotes' cry
the gong
struck from the lake's bell bottom

where the kraken
and legendary walleyes half awaken.

Long
gray afternoons
fraternal sweat and chill
six-packs and ham on rye
homeward at nightfall
from the fishing camp
aching and damp
small catch strung gill to gill.

1987

RADIO MUSIC

You flick the radio on
the habitual dial setting
and hear nothing
a measured glow
count-slowly-to-ten nothing
throb-of-the-blood-in-your-ears
nothing
empty
vacant
not even a dial tone
and know
without hesitation
that you are listening to music.

Pianissimo? Forte?
Melodious or discordant
what you hear is pause
rest
structured interval
silence
the all-enabling
indispensable bridge
counted mutely

fulcrum between recall
and anticipation
words mere noises
without juncture

music happening mainly
between the notes
riding a memory
reaching for what
will be
resolved
or broken.

This space
this gap
this hush
on which you have happened
commands the ears of others
rises or plunges
curved, spiral, or zigzag
linear or woven.

Nothing.

The dancer has run
into the wings
and the radiance on the boards
waits.

The aerialist
floats between two trapezes
invisible
till a hand catches
the bar.

1987

PAINTER OF FLOWERS

Margaret Mee 1908-1988. *In Search of Flowers of the Amazon Forests.*

The painter of flowers reenters the jungle alone
with only her brushes, her colors, her parchment, her
vow
to record the unknown, every blossom, the rarer the
better,
the fragile, the fabled, the toughly aggressive infested
with scorpions, spiders, and serpents. She paints in a
trance
by flashlight, by moonlight, by instinct by truth and
despair
the night-blooming cactus that opens once only by
darkness
that opens as though to a music unfolding a perfume
to summon the hawkmoth its soul-mate then closing
forever.

She painted by moonlight and, while she was painting,
the chain saws
were leveling trees at the ankle. The burners of charcoal
were rendering flesh of the planet aloft as a poison
eroding the air and the weather, undoing the order
on which every breather depends. And the painter of
flowers
has died and the flowers she painted, extinct, linger only

in pictures unfolding no perfume, no moth
to renew them.

1988

CONTAINER

Year of the rat? Year of the pheasant?
What emblem designates the present?

Irrational, we grow insaner
in this, the year of the CONTAINER.

In cardboard, oatmeal fed the nation
but now in plastic imitation.

Vitamins bottled, triple packed,
sit tight, a useless artifact.

Journals defy the postal carrier
by gleaming through a plastic barrier.

And have you noticed how we grapple
with plastic skin on every apple?

To render products tamper-proof
we raise a carbon-bonded roof

where two by two—contained—we dwell
engulfed by heat without emission,
the oddest ark to ring the sun,
a do it our selves sort of hell,
though slower than atomic fission,
equally sure to cook us done.

1988

PATRIOT

To be a patriot, learn to lie
when Congress asks the questions.
Take orders for a secret war
from winks and vague suggestions.

Make tax deductible appeals.
Go arms-for-Ayatolling,
and when a foreign journal squeals,
set all the shredders rolling.

Your lecture circuit is hot-wired.
The charges drop to zero.
Your president (although you're fired)
pronounces you a hero.

1989

HIGHWAY 10, MINNESOTA

By imperceptible degrees
on sky-wide steppes the road ascends
past grain, grass, hedgerows, isles of trees.
An undulant horizon bends
loosely about us as we reach
each buried sandbar that contains
the glacial Agassiz that drains
from beach to prehistoric beach.

The four-laned ribbon we pursue,
the tug when hot-breathed semis pass,
the silvered wood, the cattail slough,
the blade and plume of roadside grass—
we mark, and pavement hieroglyphs
ambiguous, not to be woke
by fear or hunger, and the whiffs
of skunk, or scentless prairie smoke.

North by northeast we cross a line
invisible but atlas sure
that rims the citadel of pine,
spruce, fir, and tamarack. Does moor-
land always have this trick of height,
the knolls and hollows thrust aloft,
sky never further than a kite
string measures? Nothing frail or soft
thrives here but blueberry, morel,
mocassin flowers random sprung
frustrate the gatherer and tell
what wintry forage may be wrung
from lean, thin-skinned, astringent ground,
the sky adjacent . . . and profound.

1989

WAFFLE IRON

The old waffle iron
with the four Duncan Phyfe feet
the striped fabric cord
black and white woven
the coiled spring hinge

nickleplated bivalve
electric heirloom—

once
before I was born
my father
on his own
baked a plain cake in it,
which had to be scraped,

the interior grid,
darkened forever.

But oh the steaming crevice
the interior miracle
nudging the hinged top
fragrance exhaling

and how the indented
circle crisply quartered
clung to the top jaw

until teased loose
with a wooden fork
and duly apportioned.

From the tarnished oyster
feast upon feast
golden medallions
preferable to pearls.

1989

THE BAD QUARTO

The bad quarto frequents waterfront bars
hangs out with disreputable types
(that kernless font)
drinks deeply
wipes its mouth
with the back of a hand—branded—
a finger short
mutters unintelligibly
(ever conning its neck verse).

The bad quarto
was dictated
in a dank warehouse
with a chorus of wharf-rats
by a drunken extra
cashiered for missing cues
to a scribe sinister
clawfoot hid in a boot.

Problematically dated
chain lines indistinct
the watermark of the scorpion
the bad quarto
on a foggy night
lurks in an alley
lunges out of an alcove
"Your money or your life!"

Auctioned at Christy's
the bad quarto
for an undisclosed price
goes to an eminent Wall-Streeter
dabbler in futures
sure to appreciate.

The bad quarto
was found in sodden wool
in the greatcoat pocket
of a drowned man in the morgue

. . . found behind plaster
in a wall undergoing demolition
. . . found uncatalogued
in a monastic library
bound with a pair of brimstone sermons.

Rife with error
the bad quarto
furnishes a dozen lines
give or take—willy-nilly—
unavailable elsewhere

on the authority of which
half a dozen experts
cloistered in colleges
pampered in conference centers
(cocktails and saunas)
would stake their illusions.

1989

FLOOD TREES

Trees wearing ankle bracelets wrought of ice
wade patiently, watching the level fall,
these ancient monopeds whose deep recall
is total: flood by flood, the height, the price,
and how the intervening years entice
bipedal builders into urban sprawl,
their costly villas trusting in a wall
of loam, a loaf for cresting tides to slice.

The trees wade chin or waist or instep deep,
engorge their fill against another drought.
One limber sapling by the north bridge bank
caught in the current tries to buck and leap
like any frightened colt but can't get out
or in, the ice floes grating on its flank.

1989

VIRTUOSO

Vladimir Horowitz 1904-1989

The fingers stainless steel, the hide
antique cordovan, furrowed brow
inclined above the keys decide
which classic to unweave, endow
with antic rhythms. Octaves wide,
the palms uproot arpeggios, flung
like sleet across a blizzard, hung
like rocket bursts in slow dissolve.
Academies do not evolve
such virtuosi, demon-sent
epitomies of temperament.

Those eight times he retires, he brings
back talent riper, more profound,
sheer mind impinging on the strings.
The last note fades—no further bow,
no encore. Though applause resound,
we cannot lure him from the wings.
Who shall control the thunder now?

1989

THESE NAMES: DECEMBER 1989

Where grave these names
on what obsidian mirror
footless crevasse
what desert monolith

names hardly legion
but many
many uninducted warriors
recruits to carnage
weaponless   untrained
wearing the casual jacket
shawl   cap   apron

undrilled   unsworn
un-led they brave
the equinoctial chill
official bludgeons
machine guns
sharp shooters
torture
mass burial

these minds in flood
a Birnam wood of forearms
the banners and the chanting

they mill in squares
clamber up monuments
surge forward
retreat   regroup   return

their palms are empty
eyes   abrim with future
they improvise

their politicians   poets
their poets   politicians

their ordnance video-cameras
they hurl their naked faces
bombard our screens
the f-word *freedom*
violates our apathy

their flesh stops tanks and bullets
their dying witnessed
and then denied

along scarred walls
small loaves of bread
blossom with candles
faded by daylight

warriors
martyrs
kin

where shall we grave your names?

1989

RONDEAU FOR MUTANTS

In our designer genes we stroll
twelve-toed on incandescent sole
down beaches tarry with the broil
and stench of effluent and oil
while flood-tides from the melting pole
swill down metropolises whole.
Far inland like a star-nosed mole
discarded fuel rods till the soil.
In our designer genes
what absolution can console
the perpetrators of such toll?
Were we the virus to despoil
a breathing planet? Are we loyal
to the inherent, mindless goal
of our designer genes?

1990

HANDKERCHIEFS

Four handkerchiefs
large linen folded and knotted
into four limber dolls
strung through the head,
the boneless backs erect,
suspended
by strong black carpet thread
along one horizontal
black cordage taut
between two chair backs

doll feet grazing boards
each white toe pierced
by a black-beaded hat pin—
tweak the string
and hear them tread
toe tapster rhythms
lax arms spread
gesticulating
shuffle kick
flop to the knees,
sit, rise,
white linen ghosts.

So light a flick
along their life line sends them
into a tarantella, a pavane
or what you will
or they will.
Your hand hardly
accounts for all this virtuosity.

Aged five perhaps
enchanted or obsessed
one rainy weekend
in a rustic cabin in Maine
with parents at a conference
I trained my dancers
to a windup phonograph.

I led my troupe.
They leapt and pirouetted
shuffled and shimmied
crawled across the floor
lay charmed asleep
turned somersaults
marched on parade
bowed deeply to applause.

For hours we played
the greatest houses:
the Met, La Scala, Covent Garden
from photos in the *Victor Book*
of Opera.

Next day
rain gone, a ramble on the beach
the long drive home
counting the hillside cows,
carried to sleep
curved stairs, familiar bed.

Later
remembering my dangling playmates
I cried a bit
never as I recall
discovered where
those lightfoot dancers fled.

1990

DUCT TAPE

She dreamt she conquered the Medellin Cartel
with a Swiss army knife and a roll of duct tape
delivered them trussed and gagged
to the Pentagon.

She could flip a three-hundred-pound assailant
over her left shoulder
without gear climb a vertical wall
ride any animal from calf to camel.

Historical Note:

Her grandmother's five-inch hat pin
stamen of veils and velvet
capable of heart puncture
was applied on occasion . . . elsewhere.

The classic defense?

In those old films, hero and villain clinched
roll on the floor in wall-to-wall mayhem.
The heroine askew with one high heel
in hand prepares to crack the villain's skull—
if not the hero's.

The National Rifle Association advises
that every prudent woman own a handgun.

Women of my generation
knew that the best defense was being elsewhere;
the second best, an audience,
preferably ethnic grandmas—elbows planted
on cushioned windowsills.

"Now you, down there,
stop that this minute!"
And stop they did, slunk off . . .

before we had perfected our technique
of stepping over bodies in the street.

The former resident of this remodeled
first-floor Victorian mansion flat
with seven full-length mirrors nailed
every window shut.
On summer nights, a hundred plus,
clad only in her sweat, on clammy linen,
she listened for the chime of glass.

On night shift in New Haven in the fifties,
walking a few dim scruffy blocks, I carried
my scout knife open in my pocket.

Men grow up tasting knuckles, blood, and gravel—
liking it even.

Women? Well, they say
we scratch, pull hair, and bite like vermin.

Gentler? More timid?
Bluebeard's wife?
Or Snow-White's stepmother?

What's nature and what's nurture when
custom and media sic the glands?

She dreamt she conquered the Medellin Cartel
with a Swiss army knife and a roll of duct tape
and walked away with violets in her hair.

1990

HABEAS CORPUS

Thomas McGrath 1916-1990

Your student mentions (brushing middle age)
that when you died
you wanted to be stolen
from the toe-tagged, discreetly sheeted,
antiseptic trolley (blast the morticians!)

clam-shelled into a car trunk,
shuttled into some high-wheeled pickup,
battered van
till, bogged to the axle,
the trail demanded portage
over rock and swamp and stump and hummock
borne shoulder-high
or piggy-backed
through trackless piney pallisades

where the tall platform has been lashed aloft
where, bound in bark, you'll wait
until the ants
and owls and whippoorwills
bear you away
distribute you
forever and again.

After the poetry reading—
words you wrote or roused—
going our ways
under the gibbous moon
fortnight before your birthday
we living listeners
shrug off—civility
together
we unbury you.

1990

OUR ICEMAN'S CAPE

Our iceman wore a leather cape,
waist-length and glossy, coveted
when we played Camelot or Troy
with barrel staves and garbage lids,
with kettle helmets, birchen bows—
we Mymidons and Amazons.

Our iceman wore a leather cape,
his dingy T-shirt biceps-burst.
He swung a mighty caliper
with prongs to clench and heft the block,
an ice-pick dagger in his belt.

"Iceman," he'd shout and shove the screen.
He knew dimensions to a T
of every ice chest on the route,
how long the melting, factored in
the weather, holidays, and guests.

Our iceman wore a leather cape
and stretched a canvas canopy
to shade his load. The tailgate post
dangled a wire-coil scale to hook
the tongs. "Don't charge us for the drip."

His inky-stubbled lantern jaw,
his pendant brow, half frightened us.
(Who'd heard of acromegaly?)
But nonetheless we pled for chips:
pond ice from moss and sawdust hoards.

Our iceman wore a leather cape.
The block that rode his armored back
was beveled, neither white nor black
nor quite translucent but contained
the rock retaining wall, the birch,
pine, maple, yellow-gabled house,
the truck, the children clamoring,
borne indoors to the brass-hinged chest
where by degrees the ice forgot
them, and itself—as I do not. 1990

EVERYONE REMEMBERS

Everyone remembers one Bette Davis movie,
if not the same, if not the name, intensely, unreliably.
Where, when, and even who played lead elude me.
Whoever starred, it was a Davis film.

This aging femme fatale has kept her—daughter?
or younger sister?—rompered and in pigtails,
herself, unaging, squired by younger men
till she falls off a yacht. Pneumonia.
Survives.

Finale: dressing table mirror—
her face has crumpled: thirty-five
to maybe seventy. She does not cry.
Her trembling hands apply
false eyelashes—like sooty moths, mascara,
and rouge (a clownish mask) a golden wig,
a satin robe, high heels.

Between a slim cane and the balustrade
beauty descends the staircase. No one dare
inform Milady. No one tries.
A queen of hearts, an amorous confection,
she totters towards the pitiless reflection
in her young lover's eyes.

1990

SEVENTY-NINE

At seventy-nine, her table blue with African violets,
she watches the scarlet amaryllis shooting up its second
  stalk
and begins piano lessons.

> "I'm playing the same simple pieces I played
>   as a child
> but I'm doing them right."

Last summer she visited Ireland and Scotland.
Soon she will be eighty.

1991

AIR SHAFT: THE FIFTIES

The air shaft was our commons. Tenants shared
and shared alike that narrow, sky-capped space,
lived hand to mouth and marginally, fared
as ingenuity allowed—or grace.
Underwear dried on ledges. Blankets aired,
and dingy windows billowed threadbare lace.
Geraniums and cushioned elbows flourished,
and grandmas supervised our storied maze,
deplored our morals. Hermits, undernourished,
knew when a lucky neighbor lifted praise
for cabbage, sweet-sour pork, or barbecue,
or floor-crossed lovers meshed a mutual gaze:
who quarreled together and who wept alone,
who worked, who idled, who coughed half the night—
always somewhere the smoky throaty moan
of some . . . professional? or no, not quite,
forever noodling on a saxophone,
distilling blues out of the urban blight.

1991

CIVIL WAR PHOTOS

After the war
obsessively photographed,
camp-follower camera
hooded on its tripod
trap with the slow shutter
soul collector
recording dignity, poise,
serenity, bravado,
passions oddly congealed
men, horses, fences,
tents, scorched chimneys, corpses,

after the war
think of those plates unvalued
silver-matted glass
smashed into landfill rubble
discounted to florists
to be soldered into lead frames
for greenhouse roofing.

Records of dead and living
images fade by the moment
gnawed by indifferent sun

nor could contrive to etch
on hybridized petals
    as Apollo in grief and guilt
    initialed the hyacinth *alas, alas*
their image of perennial grief.

1991

HEARING RUFFED GROUSE

The Stradivarius of drumming logs
encased in a burr oak thicket overgrown
with hazel, hawthorn, blueberry, and fern
tuned by the termite, gnawing ant, and worm
bridges a rotted stump, a lichened stone;
balanced, a handsbreadth underneath, the sound
undamped; limb-lopped, debarked and parched and
    pelted,
frozen and drifted level, thawed and dried,
the excavated heart, the chambered cells
ripened to new sonority, transmuted,
seasoned to richer timbre. Ears await
the virtuoso in the tweedy cape,
we misconstrued last year—not after all
spring thunder, not the bittern's hollow call,
nor pump-house motor lagging to a stall,
nor dribbling out-of-bounds a basket ball,
nor lost bassoonist—better understood
by tamarack and pine and brook and bog.
The leaping, whirling maestro of the log
joins the concerto grosso of the wood,
each movement ruffled to a dying fall.

1991

FIRST QUILT

For Cindy Palmer, Lecture &
Dialogue 25 June 1991

She made her first quilt at seventeen
her wedding quilt
later losing count:
the household quilts, the giveaways,
the quilting bees for missions.

Each child took one to college.
"Mama's eyes"
a daughter called her pattern
folding it into the drawer
before a date.

She knew the classics:
cat track and snail track,
adapted
adding a curlicue
a bar, an angle,
matching such colors
as you might not think
could blend
with such kaleidoscopic energy.

Her last quilt finished
at eight-nine
she died.

The first, the wedding quilt—
from leftovers of sewing
and the best parts of worn-outs—
who would have thought
a mere child capable

of spinning denim planets
on poplin, percale, chambray, calico,
gingham, twill, muslin:
sheer talent
such promise, thwarted—or kept?

1991

THE CAFETERIA OF THE DAMNED

In the cafeteria of the damned
The line moves slowly,
the tray oblong
composite of glue and sawdust
warped and edge-bitten,
the sole utensil
a knife
always dull.

Behind sloping glass, the salads inaccessible,
you must beg for half an egg on freckled lettuce
the quivering red jell on the leprous cabbage
the two slivers of celery, one stuffed olive, and
beetle, dead or alive.
The soup, rainwater
floating a wisp of pond weed
and two small pasta shells,
or gray as putty,
comes in a cracked bowl
with a thumb in the brim.

The meat choices,
all breaded—
oblong, triangular, square—
otherwise indistinguishable,
the vegetable side dish—
blotting paper, erasers,
or chopped rubber band—
stews in a mucoid sauce.
The coffee, tepid
brews in a sump pump.

At the cafeteria of the damned
you sit alone or share
with a vertical newspaper
in a language you do not read.
The pedestal table accommodates
three knees at most.
When you try to carve,
grating on bone,

the coffee sloshes—
your tray awash
in beverage, soup,
and the leaking roof
you have just noticed.

A pressed aluminum ceiling
suspended, imminent,
the walls flaking asbestos,
beginning to buckle, display
the head of a moth-eaten moose
a scenic calendar
an exhausted fire extinguisher
and a fly swatter.

The music, formerly Welk,
is excavating a groove
deep in a dead record.
All systems whine.

You reach for your wallet.
Your pocket
is empty.
The dire cashier
of the dark-rooted platinum hair
and perennial sneer
waves you back into line.

1991

THE BENCH

At the corner of Holdredge and North 29th
where an Omaha Cyclone Fence blocks the
playground
under the worm-eaten barrel trunk
of an up-on-its-toes curly-rooted hackberry

In Honor of John Funk
Custodian
By the Clinton PTA

says the corroded plate
sunk in the concrete slab
in the April mud
under the metal frame
of the bold blue park bench
the weathered paint flaking
the top board split
but durable
with a comforting spinal curve
available
in storm or summer shade
at the faithful bus stop
in Lincoln, Nebraska.

1992